Instruments and Music

Percussion

Daniel Nunn

Heinemann Library
Chicago, Illinois

www.heinemannraintree.com
Visit our website to find out more information about Heinemann-Raintree books.

To order:
☎ Phone 888-454-2279
💻 Visit www.heinemannraintree.com to browse our catalog and order online.

© 2012 Heinemann Library
an imprint of Capstone Global Library, LLC
Chicago, Illinois

Edited by Dan Nunn, Rebecca Rissman, and Sian Smith
Designed by Joanna Hinton-Malivoire
Picture research by Mica Brancic
Production by Victoria Fitzgerald
Originated by Capstone Global Library Ltd
Printed and bound in China by Leo Paper Products Ltd

15 14 13 12 11
10 9 8 7 6 5 4 3 2 1

Library of Congress Cataloging-in-Publication Data
Nunn, Daniel.
  Percussion / Daniel Nunn.
     p. cm.—(Instruments and music)
  Includes bibliographical references and index.
  ISBN 978-1-4329-5060-6 (hc)—ISBN 978-1-4329-5067-5 (pb)
1. Percussion instruments—Juvenile literature. I. Title.
  ML1030.N86 2012
  786.8'19—dc22   2010044781

Acknowledgments
We would like to thank the following for permission to reproduce photographs: Alamy pp. 6 (© Lebrecht Music and Arts Photo Library/Chris Stock), 20 (© Paolo Negri); © Capstone Publishers pp. 21 (Karon Dubke), 22 (Karon Dubke); Corbis p. 15 (© John Wilkes Studio); Getty Images p. 19 (OJO Images/Maria Teijeiro); Photolibrary pp. 4 (Glow Images, Inc.), 5 bottom left (© Photos India RF), 7 (Robert Harding Travel/Wally Herbert), 8 (Loop Images/Alex Hare), 10 (Hemis), 11 (Visions LLC), 12 (DK Stock/David Deas), 13 (White/Thomas Northcut), 14 (Superstock/Robert Huberman), 16 (Robert Harding Travel/Wally Herbert), 23 top (imagebroker.net/Sarah Peters), 23 bottom (Visions LLC); Shutterstock pp. 5 top left (© Tkemot), 5 top right (© Grublee), 5 bottom right (© Bhathaway), 9 (© Jorge R. Gonzalez), 17 (© Muellek Josef), 18 (© Criben).

Cover photograph of a male choir accompanied by percussion instruments in Lamu, Kenya, reproduced with permission of Corbis (JAI/ © Nigel Pavitt). Back cover photograph of a Buddhist monk and a gong, in Laos reproduced with permission of Shutterstock (© Muellek Josef).

We would like to thank Jenny Johnson, Nancy Harris, Dee Reid, and Diana Bentley for their assistance in the preparation of this book.

Every effort has been made to contact copyright holders of material reproduced in this book. Any omissions will be rectified in subsequent printings if notice is given to the publisher.

Contents

Percussion Instruments

cymbal

clarinet

People play many instruments to make music.

People bang, shake, or rub percussion instruments to make music.

Some percussion instruments can play a tune.

tabla

Some percussion instruments are used to keep rhythm.

Banging Instruments

drumstick

You bang a bass drum with a drumstick.

mallet

You bang a xylophone with a mallet.

You bang two cymbals together.

You bang bongo drums with
your hands.

Shaking Instruments

You shake maracas to make a noise.

You shake a tambourine to make
a noise.

You shake a handbell to make a noise.

You don't shake or hit windchimes at all. The wind does it for you!

Playing Percussion Instruments

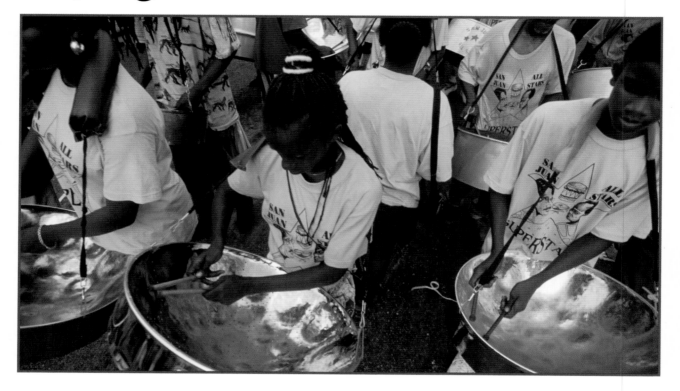

Some people play percussion instruments together.

Some people play percussion instruments on their own.

Some people play percussion instruments for work.

Some people play percussion
instruments just for fun!

Making Percussion Instruments

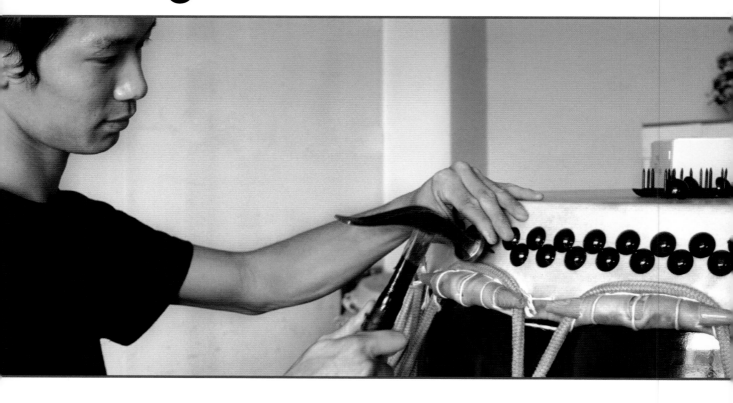

Some percussion instruments are hard to make.

Some percussion instruments are easy to make.

Play Your Own Percussion Instrument

You can play your own percussion instruments, too!

Picture Glossary

 **mallet** stick used to play some percussion instruments

 **rhythm** repeated pattern of sound

Index

Notes for Parents and Teachers

Before reading

Find examples of percussion instruments to share with the children. Online examples with audio can be found at: http://www.sfskids.org/templates/instorchframe.asp?pageid=3. Children can take turns choosing a percussion instrument and try playing it. Explain that many percussion instruments are shaken, rubbed, hit, or scraped to make sound. Can they name any of the instruments they see online?

After reading

Encourage the children to make their own percussion instruments. Ask them to fill some containers with rice or pasta, and then shake them to make their own maracas. Help them to stretch a balloon over a container to make their own drum.

Extra information

The instruments shown on page 5 are: triangle (top left), tambourine (top right), maracas (bottom right), and tabla, a type of hand drum (bottom left).

Some percussion instruments are pitched (like a xylophone) and some are unpitched (like a drum). You can play a tune on a pitched percussion instrument. You will find percussion instruments in most styles of music. They generally keep the other instruments in time and at a regular speed.